REAL-LIFE DISASTERS

INVESTIGATE WHAT <u>REALLY</u> HAPPENED!

Written by	Susan Martineau
Designed & illustrated by	Vicky Barker

www.bsmall.co.uk

Published by b small publishing ltd. www.bsmall.co.uk © b small publishing ltd. 2020 • 1 2 3 4 5 • ISBN 978-1-912909-27-8 •
Publisher: Sam Hutchinson. Art director: Vicky Barker. Editorial: Rudi Haig. Production: Madeleine Ehm. Printed in China by WKT Co. Ltd.

DISASTER DOSSIER
Real-life Disasters

When we hear about disasters we feel scared. It is only natural to feel this way. The idea of being in a disaster ourselves is terrifying. That is why it is so important to understand how disasters have happened, and to find out how they can be prevented in the future.

Read the incredible stories of the disasters first. Then look at the DISASTER DOSSIER for each one. You will be able to examine the facts behind what really happened and follow in the footsteps of the experts who investigate and try to predict or prevent disasters.

Disasters can be natural or man-made. Examples of natural disasters are earthquakes, volcanic eruptions or hurricanes. Man-made disasters happen because of something humans have done.

Investigating and understanding

After a disaster, experts are called in to investigate what has happened and why. This can take many years of gathering evidence and talking to survivors. These experts might include volcanologists who study volcanoes, meteorologists who track the weather, or historians who look into disasters of the past.

Experts also try to predict when natural disasters are going to happen. This can save many lives, but you will see that some disasters are easier to predict than others. Perhaps you will want to become one of these experts yourself?

After man-made or natural disasters, new rules are often made to keep people safe. For example, children in some countries learn at school how to survive an earthquake or a tornado.

Eyewitness statements

Disaster investigators must always be very careful to interview the people who have been through a disaster or witnessed one. They may find out vital clues about what happened and why. What questions would you ask?

Locations

The maps on the dossiers will show you where these disasters happened. Are some places in the world more likely to experience disaster than others?

Disaster Word

There is a complete list of the disaster words used in the book on the final page.

FURTHER INVESTIGATIONS
You might think of another disaster to investigate. You could write your own DISASTER DOSSIER!

perilous

annihilate

The Unsinkable Ship

On 10 April 1912, the majestic *Titanic* set sail on her first ever voyage from England to New York. She was not only the largest steamship in the world at that time, but also one of the most luxurious. For the passengers travelling in First Class, there were elegant cabins and dining rooms, and a beautiful, sweeping staircase with gold-plated crystal lights. Such a ship seemed unsinkable!

As the *Titanic* was crossing the Atlantic Ocean on Sunday, 14 April, the captain began to receive messages from other ships in the area. They warned him to beware of icebergs, but Captain Smith decided not to slow down.

At 11.40 p.m. that night, one of the sailors on lookout duty spotted an iceberg! He quickly rang the warning bell. First Officer William Murdoch gave the order to steer away from the berg and to put the engines into reverse.

But it was too late! Seconds later the iceberg ripped into the hull of the ship and water began to pour in. By midnight, the captain gave the order to launch the lifeboats. Families were split up as women and children were given places in the boats first.

Just after two o'clock in the morning, the terrified passengers on the lifeboats watched in horror as the stern (back) of the ship reared high into the air. Hundreds of people still clinging to the ship fell into the ocean to die of hypothermia in the freezing water. Finally, the huge ship broke in half and then plunged beneath the waves.

Hours later the cold, exhausted survivors were rescued by another ship, the *Carpathia*. On board, a lucky few were reunited with loved ones they thought they had lost for ever. But two thirds of all the people on board the *Titanic* had died. How could such a magnificent, 'unsinkable' ship have come to such a tragic end?

Turn over to read the **disaster dossier** ...

TITANIC DISASTER DOSSIER

... Turn back to read the story of the disaster.

Location

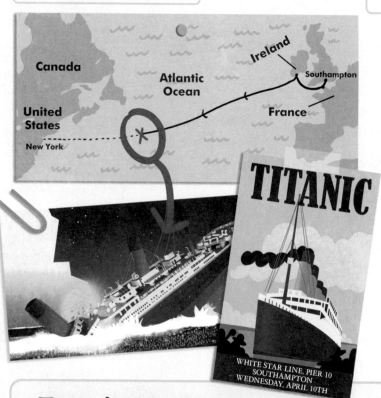

Canada

Atlantic Ocean

Ireland

Southampton

United States

France

New York

Timeline of sinking

14 April **11.40 p.m.**	Iceberg spotted by lookout. Collision with berg.
15 April **12.45 a.m.**	Lifeboats launched.
15 April **2.18 a.m.**	Bow (front) of ship sinks underwater. Ship breaks up.
15 April **2.20 a.m.**	Stern (back) rises up into air. *Titanic* sinks completely.
15 April **4.10 a.m.**	First lifeboats seen by *Carpathia*.
15 April **8.30 a.m.**	Last survivors rescued by *Carpathia*.

TITANIC

WHITE STAR LINE, PIER 10
SOUTHAMPTON
WEDNESDAY, APRIL 10TH

Eyewitness statements

'The boats were being only partly filled, their capacity being about 65 and they were being loaded with about 30 or 40 people.'

'I saw the masses of people who had backed steadily toward the stern of the big ship as her nose slowly sank, fall into the ocean as the vessel went up on end and disappeared beneath the water.'

John B. Thayer Jr, who jumped into the ocean and was pulled on to an overturned lifeboat.

'An officer was shouting, "Come on here, lively now, this way, women and children," and before I knew what was happening we were in a lifeboat ... while the men stood back serious and sober, watching us.'

Mrs Wells, a passenger in Second Class

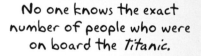

TITANIC SINKING
NO LIVES LOST

Some newspapers got it wrong!

April 16th 1912

TITANIC DISASTER GREAT LOSS OF LIFE

DEATHS AND SURVIVORS

No one knows the exact number of people who were on board the *Titanic*.

* Some people with tickets may not have turned up for the trip.

* Maybe there were a few stowaways!

* About 1,500 people died.

* 706 were rescued.

Why did so many people die?

* There were not enough lifeboats for everyone.

* Lifeboats were launched before they were full.

* There was no lifeboat drill. Passengers did not know what to do.

* Only one ship came to the rescue.

Investigating and understanding

Design of the ship

* The hull had 16 compartments. There were dividing walls called bulkheads between each one. The shipbuilders said the ship would not sink, even if four compartments were flooded.

* BUT five of the compartments were damaged by the collision AND there were gaps at the top of the bulkheads. Water flooded over them, like an over-full ice-cube tray.

Speed and steering

* The US Senate held an enquiry and blamed Captain Smith for ignoring iceberg warnings and steaming ahead through the icefield.

* The ship was so huge that it took too long to steer away from the iceberg.

Saving lives

In 1913, new rules were made at the International Conference for Safety of Life at Sea.

INTERNATIONAL CONFERENCE FOR SAFETY OF LIFE AT SEA, • 1913 •

*There **MUST** be a lifeboat space for every passenger on a ship and lifeboat drills on every voyage.

* There **MUST** be a 24-hour radio watch to make sure distress signals were always picked up by other ships in the area.

* An International Ice Patrol was set up. This patrol still warns ships of icebergs in the North Atlantic today.

FOLLOW THE EXPERTS ...

STRANGE STORIES

After the disaster, stories were told about people having premonitions or foreseeing the disaster. Some even said the ship had been cursed.

Evidence from the wreck

* In 1985, oceanographer and deep-sea archaeologist Robert Ballard found the wreck of the *Titanic*.

* Instead of one big hole in the hull, scientists saw several thin gashes. It also looked like the metal plates of the hull had split apart.

* Examination of metal samples showed that the metal used was not strong enough to stand up to an icefield full of icebergs.

Disaster Word
hypothermia

This is when you get so cold it can kill you. The icy water caused death within 15-30 minutes.

Shaking Planet

The ground we walk on looks solid, but there are many places on our planet where the earth sometimes shakes and causes terrible disasters. In 1906, a huge earthquake shook the city of San Francisco in California, USA. People were peacefully sleeping in their beds when their homes began to shake violently.

Chimneys crashed down from rooftops, houses crumpled and all the church bells in the city started to clang. People were trapped inside falling buildings and many were killed. Gas pipes were broken and fires broke out. The city began to burn in a terrible fire that lasted for three days. Over half of the people in the city lost their homes. It is hard to know just how many people died in the disaster, because even the records at City Hall were destroyed.

Fires often break out after earthquakes and make the disaster even worse. However, these are not the only dangers. Sometimes an earthquake creates giant waves, or tsunamis, which sweep away buildings and people.

On 1 November 1755, the people of Lisbon, Portugal, were in church to celebrate the Feast of All Saints. At around nine o'clock in the morning a huge earthquake shook the city. Everyone rushed out of the churches and cathedrals which were crashing down all around them. They dashed down to the shore where they thought they would be safer.

Strangely, the sea had drawn right back from the coast.
The Lisbon townspeople were astonished to see old shipwrecks
and fish flapping about on the seabed. However, little did
they know that this meant they were in deadly danger.
Within minutes, a giant tsunami swept thousands of
people away. Huge waves battered not only Portugal,
but also Spain and North Africa.

In Japan, an earthquake
not only caused a series
of tsunamis, but also
massive landslides.
The Great Kanto
Earthquake of 1923
destroyed the cities of
Tokyo and Yokohama
and the surrounding
countryside. A whole
mountainside collapsed.
It pushed an entire
village, including a
station and a train full of
passengers, into the sea.

Earthquakes can
devastate huge areas and
kill thousands of people.
Can these disasters ever
be predicted?

Turn over to read the **disaster dossier** ...

EARTHQUAKE DISASTER DOSSIER

... Turn back to read the story of the disaster.

Locations

San Francisco Quake

Date:
18 April 1906

Deaths:
At least 3,000
people killed

'I heard a low distant rumble.
It was coming from the west,
louder and louder. ... Then it hit.
Power and trolley lines snapped
like threads. The ends of the power
lines dropped to the pavement
not 10 feet from where I stood,
writhing and hissing like reptiles.
Brick and glass showered
about me.'

**Thomas Jefferson Chase,
ferry ticket clerk**

Lisbon Quake

Date:
1 November 1755

Deaths:
Up to 60,000 people killed
(in Portugal and also Spain
and Morocco)

'... this dismal earthquake had
such an influence upon the sea and
river, that the water rose, in about
ten minutes, several yards
perpendicular ... with a cry that
the sea was coming in, all people
crowded forward to run to the
hills ...'

**British merchant's
letter to his brother**

Great Kanto Quake

Date:
1 September 1923

Deaths:
At least 140,000
people killed

'To stand or walk was a physical
impossibility. Those who did not
crouch in terror the instant the
shock began were thrown violently
to the ground. The earth split and
cracked in all directions ...'

**W.D. Cameron,
Canadian businessman
in Yokohama**

The Call=Chronicle=Examiner

SAN FRANCISCO, THURSDAY, APRIL 19, 1906

EARTHQUAKE AND FIRE: SAN FRANCISCO IN RUINS

Why does the earth shake?

The Earth's surface is made of huge slabs of rock called tectonic plates. These are constantly moving. An area called a fault line is formed where two plates slip past each other.

Sometimes the edges of two plates in a fault line get stuck as they are trying to slide past each other. They keep trying to move and this stores up energy in the rock edges.

When the plates finally 'unstick', the stored energy spreads out in shock waves called seismic waves. They shake the earth!

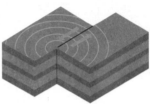

Investigating and predicting

* Seismologists are scientists who study earthquakes. They use special instruments called seismometers to measure the shock waves from earthquakes.

* Seismometers record even the smallest earthquakes all over the world. There are about 500,000 DETECTABLE earthquakes every year!

* Scientists also track the movements of tectonic plates using GPS (Global Positioning System). They monitor fault lines and build up a picture of where most earthquakes seem to happen and how powerful they are.

BUT

It is impossible to predict exactly WHEN there will be a major earthquake.

Saving lives

* Earthquakes smash down buildings and kill many people. As the world's population grows, more and more people will be living in earthquake zones. Buildings must be built to sway instead of fall down during a quake.

* Schoolchildren in parts of the world where there is a risk of an earthquake do a special earthquake drill.

DROP! **COVER!** **HOLD ON!**

* If you are outside: get away from buildings, streetlights and overhead wires.

FOLLOW THE EXPERTS ...

Disaster Word
devastate
means to destroy completely.

Life-saving facts

* In 2004, there was a terrible tsunami in South East Asia. A young girl called Tilly Smith was on a beach when she saw the sea was going out really far. She had just learnt about tsunamis at school. She knew that as the big wave reaches the shore it grows higher, but the trough before the wave pulls water away from the shore first. Tilly shouted to everyone to run away from the beach before the big wave arrived. She saved many lives that day.

Tsunami danger!

* Sometimes there are earthquakes under the oceans. These can cause massive waves of water called tsunamis (soo-na-mees). Seismologists have set up warning systems in some parts of the world. If an underwater quake is detected, they can warn people to get to safety before a tsunami hits.

Dino Disaster

Dinosaurs lived happily on Planet Earth for more than 100 million years. Most of them died out suddenly about 66 million years ago. Even though this is a very, very, very long time ago, scientists think they may know how nearly all the dinosaurs were wiped out.

There is a gigantic crater on the coast of Mexico. It was made by a monster rock from outer space whacking into the surface of our planet. It must have been a terrifying sight. As it smashed into Earth, the rock made giant clouds of ash and dust fly up into the atmosphere. These blotted out the light from the Sun for years. The planet became dark and cold.

Plants and trees need sunlight to grow. Without sunlight they die and no new plants or trees grow either. The poor vegetarian dinosaurs (herbivores) would have had nothing left to eat. They would have starved to death. At first, the meat-eaters (carnivores) would have eaten all the herbivores, but soon there would have been no food for them to chomp on either! It was a disaster for the dinosaurs.

But this is not the only mega-rock to have landed on Earth from space. In the Arizona Desert in the USA, there is another enormous crater. You could fit nearly three Empire State Buildings end-to-end across it. Scientists think it is about 50,000 years old.

In 1908, a mysterious object exploded in the skies above Siberia in Russia. It is such a remote area that there were not many people living there. The closest people to the explosion were some reindeer herders. They were in their tents about 30 km (20 miles) away and were blown into the air and knocked unconscious. The forest around them burst into flames and many reindeer died. People who lived hundreds of kilometres away saw a huge fireball in the sky and heard deafening bangs.

There are thousands of rocks whizzing around in space and, luckily, big ones do not smash into Earth very often. In 1996, one of them missed our planet by only 450,000 km (279,000 miles). This sounds like a long way away, but it is not much further than from here to the Moon. We don't want to end up like the poor old dinosaurs!

Turn over to read the **disaster dossier** ...

SPACE ROCK DISASTER DOSSIER

... Turn back to read the story of the disaster.

Locations

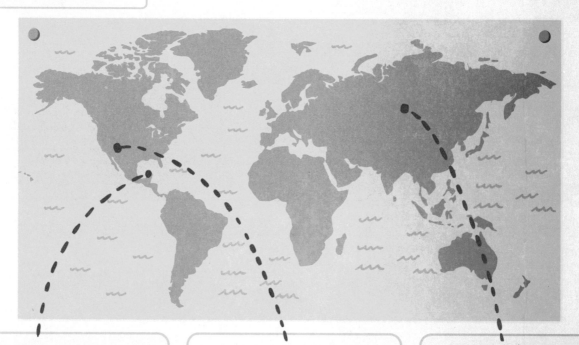

Dinosaur Killer Rock

Chicxulub,
Yucatan Peninsula,
Mexico

Space rock landed:
Between 65 and 66
million years ago

Size of crater:
180 km (112 miles) wide

NO HUMAN WITNESSES

Arizona Mega-rock

Winslow, Arizona, USA

Space rock landed:
50,000
years ago

Size of crater:
1,200 metres
(4,000 feet) wide

NO HUMAN WITNESSES

Siberian Fireball

Tunguska, Siberia,
Russia

Date of explosion
30 June 1908

Size of crater:
No crater but massive
destruction of forest

Eyewitness statements

'Everything around was shrouded in smoke
and fog from the burning fallen trees.
... Many reindeer rushed away and were lost.'
Reindeer herder, Siberia

'... high above the forest the whole northern part of
the sky appeared covered with fire. ... At that moment
there was a bang in the sky, and a mighty crash.
... The crash was followed by a noise like stones
falling from the sky, or guns firing.'
Witness, 60 km (37 miles) away

What are space rocks?

* **Asteroids** are made of rock. They can be hundreds of kilometres across, or as small as pebbles.

* **Comets** are balls of ice, rock and dust with long tails of gas and dust. They are the size of a small town!

Investigating and understanding

* Fossil scientists (palaeontologists) have worked out that most of the dinosaurs became extinct around 66 million years ago. Scientists who study the rocks on Earth (geologists) say the Chicxulub Crater in Mexico was made by a large asteroid or comet around the same time.

* Geologists have also discovered a metal called iridium in rock layers dating from 66 million years ago. Iridium is very rare on Earth, but it IS found in space rocks. When the Chicxulub space rock exploded on Earth's surface it would have covered a huge area of the world with iridium.

* Other scientists think that the disaster was not only caused by a space rock. There were also lots of disastrous volcanic eruptions on Earth at around that time.

Predicting and preventing

* Astronomers are scientists who study space. Some of them watch the skies for big asteroids and comets that might come too close to Earth. Luckily for us these are quite rare!

* Scientists are experimenting with ways of stopping a very large rock from smashing into our planet. One idea is to use rockets to knock an asteroid into a different path, or orbit, so that it does not threaten Earth.

FOLLOW THE EXPERTS ...

Disaster Word

extinction

means dying out completely. If a species of animal is extinct it means there is not one of them left alive in the whole world.

STRANGE STORIES!

Some people say that the Tunguska fireball was an alien spaceship coming to land on Earth! But scientists believe it was an asteroid that exploded in Earth's atmosphere. That is why people saw a burning ball of fire in the sky.

The Treacherous Triangle

The oceans of the world are huge and beautiful. Many ships and planes travel across them every day. Most of them cross safely, but oceans can also be dangerous places. There is one area of the Atlantic Ocean where many ships and planes have disappeared. In 1964, a journalist called Vincent Gaddis invented a name for this area. He called it 'The Bermuda Triangle', and he said that there was something strange and mysterious about these disasters.

An American ship, the USS *Cyclops*, is just one of the many lost ships. In March 1918, the *Cyclops* was carrying a heavy cargo when it set off from Barbados in the Caribbean. It was heading across the Atlantic Ocean towards Baltimore on the east coast of the United States. Somewhere in the 'Triangle', disaster struck. The *Cyclops* never reached its final destination. The huge ship and over 300 crew and passengers were never seen again. There was no call for help from the *Cyclops*, and no wreckage has ever been found.

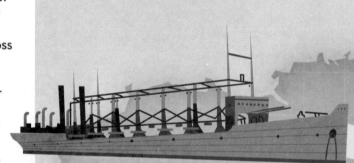

In 1945, five American Navy bomber planes set off on a training flight from their base at Fort Lauderdale in Florida. At first, everything went well, but then the planes seemed to lose their way. 'I don't know where we are,' said one of the pilots over his radio. The pilot in charge of the mission also reported, 'Both my compasses are out and I'm trying to find Fort Lauderdale.'

The confused pilots carried on flying and the planes began to run out of fuel. Back at base, no one could understand why the planes seemed to be heading further and further out across the ocean. The Navy urgently sent search planes to look for the missing aircraft. To everyone's horror, one of these rescue planes also disappeared over the ocean. Six planes had now vanished with all of their crew.

Other people have somehow survived 'The Bermuda Triangle'. In 1964, pilot Chuck Wakely saw a dazzling glow around his plane and then all his instruments went wrong. Another man, called Gerald Hawkes, said the plane he was on suddenly dropped down and then shot up again on the way to the small island of Bermuda. In 1966, a tugboat was going from Puerto Rico to Fort Lauderdale when its compass and electric power stopped working. The captain said a strange darkness came down and the waves were really high. It must have been terrifying.

BERMUDA

FORT LAUDERDALE

MIAMI

BERMUDA TRIANGLE

PUERTO RICO

Are some areas of ocean more perilous than others, or is there something more sinister going on?

Turn over to read the **disaster dossier** ...

TRIANGLE DISASTER DOSSIER

... Turn back to read the story of the disaster.

Location

United States

Bermuda

BERMUDA TRIANGLE

Miami

Cuba

Puerto Rico

MISSING IN THE TRIANGLE

About 50 ships and 20 planes.
Up to 1,000 people.
The exact number is not known.

NO WRECKAGE EVER FOUND!

Reports of unexplained disappearances started in the 1800s.

A Vanishing Ship	The Lost Planes	Missing Rescue Aircraft
Name: USS *Cyclops*	**Name:** Flight 19	**Name:** Mariner flying boat
Number of crew and passengers: 309	**Number of planes:** 5	**Number of crew:** 13
Date disappeared: Some time after 4 March 1918	**Number of crew:** 14	**Date disappeared:** 5 December 1945
	Date disappeared: 5 December 1945	

Eyewitness statements

'It was as if a giant hand was holding the plane and jerking it up and down ... time and space seemed to disappear.'

Gerald Hawkes,
on a plane going to Bermuda

'The water seemed to be coming from all directions.'

Don Henry, captain of the tugboat

THE DEADLY BERMUDA TRIANGLE

WHO WILL BE ITS NEXT VICTIM?

The **Bermuda Triangle**
an incredible saga of unexplained disappearances
Charles Berlitz

Many books have been written about the Triangle.

THE BERMUDA TRIANGLE MYSTERY – SOLVED

What do we know so far?

* The Atlantic Ocean is HUGE. It is very difficult to find wreckage from accidents.

* This means there is no evidence to examine. Without the wreckage of the ships and planes, it is hard to investigate why they went down.

* There are many theories behind the disappearances. No one knows for sure!

Investigating and understanding

Nothing unusual here!

* The US Coastguard says there is nothing strange about the number of planes and ships going down. There are often very bad storms in the area. It is also very busy with a lot of ocean traffic.

* The *Cyclops* was overloaded. It probably sank in a massive storm.

* The US Navy said that the planes of Flight 19 got lost for 'reasons unknown'. The fuel ran out and the planes crashed into the ocean.

* The search plane crashed, because its fuel tank exploded. Some oil slicks on the ocean were spotted at the time. These could have been from the plane.

Human error?

* Compasses do not point to the geographical North at the North Pole. They point to magnetic North. The difference between these two directions depends on where you are in the world. Sailors and pilots must take this into account.

* Maybe some of the planes and boats that have disappeared were steered by people who did not have the skills to find their way, or to survive such a wild and stormy ocean.

Weirder explanations

Rogue waves

* Oceanographers (scientists who study the oceans and seas) believe that unusually high waves can appear out of nowhere in the middle of the ocean. These freak waves can be over 30 metres (100 feet) high and could easily smash up a ship.

Gas bubbles

* There is a lot of methane gas under the seabed. Could giant bubbles of gas sink ships and stop aircraft instruments from working properly? If so, this would also be happening in other areas of the oceans too.

Strange glow

* Some kinds of seaweed give off an eerie glow at night. They are covered in bioluminescent bacteria. Could this have caused the odd light effects seen by Chuck Wakely?

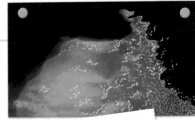

FOLLOW THE EXPERTS ...

Disaster Word

perilous

means very dangerous.

STRANGE STORIES!

Vincent Gaddis, and the authors of many other books on the Triangle, believe there is something supernatural about the disappearances. Others say there are alien spaceships under the ocean and these are capturing the planes and ships, along with their crews.

Inferno at Sea

We use a huge amount of oil and gas to power our planet and some of it is found under Earth's seas and oceans. Enormous platforms, or rigs, are used to drill and pump out these fossil fuels. The people who work on these rigs get there by helicopter. The rigs are pumping night and day, so staff work in shifts around the clock.

The Piper Alpha platform was 193 km (120 miles) off the coast of Scotland in the wild and windy North Sea. In 1988, it was the scene of the world's worst-ever oil rig disaster. Oil rigs can be dangerous places, but no one expected such a terrible tragedy.

Piper Alpha was built to pump oil but by the 1980s it was also pumping gas. It was joined, by a network of pipes, to other rigs in the North Sea. On the night of 6 July 1988, one of Piper Alpha's pumps stopped working. The night-shift workers switched on another pump and there was a sudden explosion! It ripped through the rig and was quickly followed by another deadly blast. A huge fireball whooshed high into the night sky.

Meanwhile, oil and gas were still being pumped along the pipes from the other rigs. These pipes melted and there were more explosions. Fire now spread uncontrollably throughout Piper Alpha. Desperate workers had to save themselves in any way they could. Men leapt into the sea from high up on the rig or scrambled down ropes. Rescue boats came to help and, tragically, one of these was blown up by another explosion.

There were more than 200 men on the rig that night. About 80 of them were off-duty in the accommodation block. They waited to be rescued by helicopter, but it was impossible. There was too much black smoke and immense flames shot 200 metres (655 feet) into the sky. Just before midnight the rig began to buckle and groan. The entire accommodation block slid beneath the sea. None of the men inside could be saved.

By quarter to one in the morning all that was left of Piper Alpha was a black, burning stump sticking up out of the sea. In just two hours the platform had been destroyed and many men had lost their lives. How could such a terrible disaster have happened?

Turn over to read the **disaster dossier** ...

OIL RIG DISASTER DOSSIER

... Turn back to read the story of the disaster.

Location

PIPER ALPHA PLATFORM

Claymore platform

Aberdeen

Tartan platform

Scotland

Timeline of disaster

6 July 9.45 p.m. — First pump stops working. Second pump switched on.

10.00 p.m. — First explosion, quickly followed by another blast.

10.20 p.m. — Gas pipes from nearby rigs melt. Another explosion. Fire spreads throughout Piper Alpha.

10.50 p.m. — More explosions. Rescue boat destroyed.

11.50 p.m. — Four-storey accommodation block collapses into the sea.

Eyewitness statements

'The explosion came. Next second, I'm 15 foot away up the other end of the control room.'
Geoff Bollands, control room operator, describing the first explosion.

'The last time we went to the rig, the whole world seemed to be on fire. The noise was absolutely deafening. If you could imagine a blow-torch and then magnify the sound of that blow-torch maybe three, four thousand times and you will get an idea of the noise.'
Charles Haffey, crewman on a rescue boat, who helped to rescue over 30 men (before his boat was snapped in half by an explosion).

'You wonder why people would jump out of a 30 or 40-storey block window when fire is at their back. Well, I know why now, because I jumped as well and I was very lucky to survive. When I hit the sea, I went very deep, but you could see above that the flames were lighting up the surface of the sea.'
Roy Carey, instrument technician, jumped from a height of over 20 metres (70 feet) into the sea.

DEATHS AND SURVIVORS

167 men killed (including 2 crewmen from a rescue boat).

61 survivors.

MISSION OF MERCY
The Sandhaven rushed to the scene of Piper Alpha blast

How did the fire start?

MOST LIKELY CAUSE

* When the first pump stopped working the second one was switched on. This pump was faulty.

* The night shift did not know that the day workers had not finished repairing it. It should not have been used.

* Gas leaked out and exploded. This was the first explosion.

Investigating and understanding

There was an official enquiry into the tragedy. The experts said:

* There should have been better communication between the day and night workers so that the second pump was not used.

* The rig had been built to pump oil, not gas. It had fire-proof walls, but these were not strong enough to stand up to gas explosions. The firewalls were smashed by the blasts and the fire then spread quickly throughout the whole platform.

* The control room was so badly damaged in the first explosion that it was impossible to start the rig's automatic firefighting systems.

* The other connected rigs should have stopped pumping fuel immediately.

* The accommodation block of the platform should not have been built above the pumping area.

Saving lives

* Oil rigs are dangerous places, but the brave people who work on them deserve to be as safe as possible.

* The experts involved in the enquiry came up with 106 urgent changes to make oil and gas platforms much safer in the future.

FOLLOW THE EXPERTS …

Heroes of the fire

* There were many heroes that terrible night. Twenty men received medals for their bravery in helping others to escape the inferno. Sadly, two of the medals were awarded to the families of men who had given up their own lives to save others.

Disaster Word
inferno

means a very large fire that is out of control.

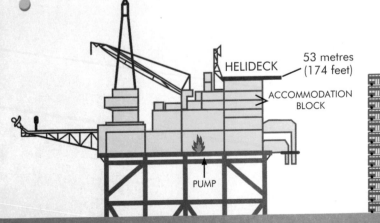

HELIDECK

53 metres (174 feet)

ACCOMMODATION BLOCK

PUMP

Height of rig = 12 double decker buses

FOR BRAVERY

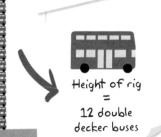

Fireball!

Airships were first invented in 1852. They were huge, torpedo-shaped aircraft with a 'balloon' full of gas to keep them up in the air. Passengers travelled in comfortable cabins and they loved the way the airships glided along, lighter than air.

On the evening of 4 October 1930, a huge airship took to the skies above England. The brand-new airship R101 was on its way to India for its first big flight. A crowd of people on the ground cheered as the ship rose into the sky. There were 54 people on board.

The passengers ate their evening meal in the airship's luxurious dining room. Then they strolled about or sat on a special viewing deck to look down below. It was like being on a cruise ship in the sky. By eight o'clock in the evening R101 was flying over London, just below the clouds.

In the days before the journey, some last-minute changes had been made to the design of the airship, but there was not enough time to test the ship at top speed or in really bad weather. There were some very important passengers from the British government travelling to India and they did not want to delay the flight. Everyone was excited about the new ship and they wanted to show it off to the world.

As the airship flew on into the night towards France, the passengers went to their cabins to sleep. The weather became very windy and rainy, although weather reports said it would improve. At 2 a.m. the captain went off duty and his second officer took control. Just minutes later the airship suddenly dived down towards the ground. People were knocked off their feet and the furniture slid around.

The crew managed to steady the airship, but it was now flying too close to the ground. It needed to get back up to a safe height. They did all they could, but the airship dived again. The crew knew they would have to make an emergency landing. 'We're down lads,' said one of them.

The airship landed safely, and the crew must have been so relieved. Then disaster struck!

The ship exploded into intense flames. Only six people survived the fireball. How could such a tragedy have happened to such a magnificent, new airship?

Turn over to read the **disaster dossier** ...

AIRSHIP DISASTER DOSSIER

... Turn back to read the story of the disaster.

Location

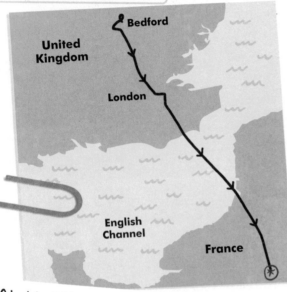

Bedford

United Kingdom

London

English Channel

France

Timeline of flight

4 October 6.36 p.m.	Airship R101 lifts off from Bedfordshire, England.
5 October 2 a.m.	Captain Irwin hands over command to Second Officer. Weather is very windy and rainy.
5 October 2.07 a.m.	Airship suddenly dives towards the ground. Crew manage to steady the ship.
5 October 2.08 a.m.	Airship dives down again. Crew crash-lands ship, but ... seconds later ... AIRSHIP EXPLODES INTO FLAMES.

Airship R101 was 3 times as long as a Boeing 747.

The gas in the airship 'balloon' was **HYDROGEN** = highly inflammable.

NUMBER OF DEAD

48 people died (including 2 who died later in hospital).

Fireball!

Eyewitness statements

'Shock of impact not great – more a crunch than a blow – I was not even shaken. Within 2 seconds of striking, a blinding flash of fire appeared to originate from above the control car. I saw the mass of flame.'

Harry Leech, Foreman Engineer, described the two dives and then the crash-landing.

He survived.

'After the explosion the sky was filled with pieces of burning wreckage and these floated away from the spot slowly sinking; it looked like a large firework going off.'

Miss Moillez, aged 14,
French girl who saw the disaster.

TERRIBLE AIR TRAGEDY

R101 CRASHES IN FLAMES

ALL AIRSHIP LEADERS LOST

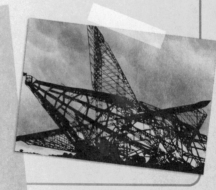

What probably happened?

Everyone on duty in the control room died. This makes it very hard to know exactly why the accident happened.

* The bad weather ripped into the front of the ship. Gas leaked out of the gasbags. This made the ship dive down.

* The crew could not stop the airship from losing height. They had to crash-land, nose first.

* The engine twisted round and set fire to the highly inflammable hydrogen gas.

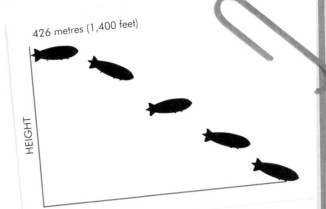

426 metres (1,400 feet)

HEIGHT

Investigating and understanding

Airship design and testing

* The design was changed to add another gasbag. This was to help the heavy ship lift into the air safely.

* The ship should then have been tested at full speed and in bad weather. This was not done before the flight to India.

* Some parts of the outer cover had been repaired before the flight. They should have been completely replaced instead. The bad weather on the flight split the cover.

Pressure to leave on time!

* The passengers included the British Air Minister, Lord Thomson, and most of the expert engineers who had designed the airship. They had all worked hard to get R101 ready for the flight.

* There were big expectations about the amazing journey so no one really wanted to delay the departure, even though they knew the airship needed more testing.

FOLLOW THE EXPERTS ...

Wind and rain

* The weather was very stormy, especially in France where the airship went down. The split would have let in rain. This would make the airship heavier and hard to keep up in the air.

* A downward gust of wind may also have forced the airship into the first dive.

Bad timing

* The captain handed over control to the second officer at 2 a.m., just before the first dive. This officer immediately had to deal with the emergency.

Disaster Word
inflammable
describes something that bursts into flames very easily, like the hydrogen gas in the airship.

STRANGE STORIES

After such a disaster, people sometimes say they had a feeling that something bad would happen. Some of these premonitions can be very spooky. One of the crew members was leaving home for the flight when his little boy began to cry, 'I haven't got a daddy'. His father did not return.

Wild Weather

Extreme weather causes some of the worst natural disasters in the world. Terrible floods and violent storms can destroy whole towns and kill many people.

Mega-storm

On 8 November 1970, a violent storm began to form over the Bay of Bengal in South Asia. It became a swirling mass of high winds (a cyclone) and it was heading towards the nearest land. Ships sent urgent messages to warn the people living on the coast that there was a terrible cyclone on its way, but many people did not get the warning in time.

The cyclone smashed into the coast of Bangladesh (then called East Pakistan) on 12 November 1970. By now the speed of the wind was a terrifying 185 kph (115 mph). The wind was so strong that it pushed masses of seawater on to the land. Bangladesh is very low-lying even compared to the normal level of the sea. This storm surge completely inundated islands and land near the coast.

The worst-hit area was a large island called Bhola. Whole villages were swept away. Hundreds of thousands of people and farm animals died in what was named the Bhola Cyclone. It was one of the deadliest cyclones ever.

Monster Twister

Stormy weather can also bring terrifying whirlwinds called tornadoes. Although they do not last for as long as cyclones, they can smash up everything in their path and even suck up water from rivers. They are like a monster vacuum cleaner ripping across the land.

On 18 March 1925, a deadly tornado ripped through three American states. It roared through towns, farms, and even across rivers, in Missouri, Illinois and Indiana. The ferocious, whirling winds obliterated whole towns. Houses blew away, trees snapped and objects were picked up and then dumped back down many kilometres away.

The tornado rampaged over a distance of 300 km (186 miles) for three and a half hours. It destroyed several towns, killed hundreds of people, and injured thousands more. The tornado was bigger and lasted for longer than any other tornado in US history.

Turn over to read the **disaster dossiers** ...

CYCLONE
DISASTER DOSSIER

TORNADO
DISASTER DOSSIER

... Turn back to read the story of the disasters.

Location of Bhola Cyclone

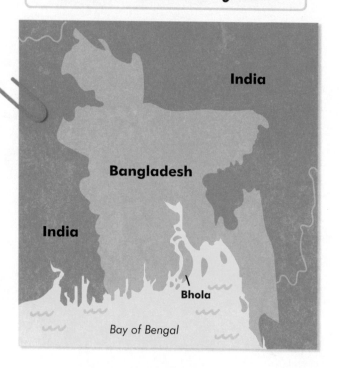

Location of the Tri-state Tornado

NUMBER OF DEATHS

Up to 500,000 people
= half a million.
But no one knows exactly
how many people died.

NUMBER OF DEATHS

Nearly 700 people died.
2,000 were injured.

Eyewitness statement

'I was clinging to a bamboo pole but a wave swept me out to sea. After six hours, at daybreak, it washed me up 15 miles away. I am the only survivor of my family.'

Modan Mohan Shaha, 18 years old.

Eyewitness statement

'There was a great roar. Like a train, but many, many times louder. ... The air was full of everything, boards, branches of trees, garments, pans, stoves, all churning around together.'

Judith Cox, who was having lunch in Gorham, Illinois.

(A cow even came through the roof of the restaurant!)

What is a cyclone?

* A **cyclone** is a violent storm with very high winds that spiral around a calmer centre or 'eye'. It forms above seas and oceans and can be 400 km (250 miles) wide.

Cyclones are also called hurricanes or typhoons.

What is a tornado?

* A **tornado** is a twisting funnel of air that can form during thunderstorms. It touches down over land and is narrower, faster and more violent than a cyclone.

Investigating and understanding

* When the Bhola Cyclone happened in 1970 it was very difficult to warn everyone in time. There were no mobile phones in those day.

* In 1925, American weather forecasters did not even use the word 'tornado'. Anyway, they were nearly impossible to predict without modern technology.

Saving lives

* Special cyclone shelters have been built in Bangladesh to keep people safer.

* People who live in certain areas of the USA know what they have to do in case of a tornado warning. Their best chance is to shelter in a basement room without windows. You cannot out-run a tornado!

Predicting wild weather

* Meteorologists are scientists who study our planet's weather. They use radar networks and satellite pictures to forecast and track storms. Weather warning systems are now used around the world to tell people when cyclones or tornadoes are likely to happen.

FOLLOW THE EXPERTS ...

Climate change danger

* The climate on Planet Earth is getting hotter and humans are making it worse. Sea levels are rising and even the ice at the North and South Poles is melting. People living in low-lying countries, like Bangladesh, are in even more danger from flooding during wild weather.

Disaster Words
inundate
means to flood an area with water.

obliterate
means to destroy completely.

The Wrecked City

During the First World War, many ships passed through the huge, sheltered harbour of Halifax, Nova Scotia. The ships carried soldiers who were going to battle. They also took essential supplies of food, fuel and weapons across the Atlantic Ocean to war-torn Europe.

On the morning of 6 December 1917, one of the ships leaving the harbour was a large, Norwegian vessel called the SS *Imo*. Its mission was to take urgent supplies to the people of Belgium. That day, another ship was just about to enter the port. It was a French ship called the SS *Mont-Blanc*. It was packed with tons of explosives and was going to join other ships returning to the war in Europe.

The captain of the *Imo* had already waited for several days in the harbour for supplies to be delivered. He set off fast, but had to keep changing course to avoid other ships in the busy waterway. Meanwhile, the *Mont-Blanc* was making its way into the harbour through the narrow entrance to the port. It was being steered by Francis Mackey, a harbour pilot.

SS *Imo*

SS *Mont-Blanc*

Mackey was shocked to see the *Imo* speeding straight towards him. Despite both ships sending out warning whistles, it was too late to avoid a collision. The *Imo* gashed a hole in the hull of the *Mont-Blanc*. This started a huge fire in the fuel drums on deck. An enormous plume of black smoke rose up into the sky. People on shore, including many children on their way to school, gathered to watch.

The crew of the *Mont-Blanc* rowed for their lives to shore and tried to tell everyone to run away. By now the burning ship, packed with 3,000 tons of explosives, was drifting towards the busiest part of Halifax. Just after nine o'clock, the *Mont-Blanc* was annihilated in a gigantic, catastrophic explosion.

Hundreds of people died instantly. The shock waves from the explosion shattered windows and doors many kilometres away. People were blown up into the air and badly injured by shards of glass. Hot gas and shrapnel rained down. Fire raged through the wooden buildings of the city. The blast also created a huge wave that devastated the shore area.

The Halifax Explosion was one of the greatest catastrophes in the history of Canada. How could a city be wrecked like this?

Turn over to read the **disaster dossier** ...

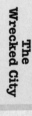

EXPLOSION DISASTER DOSSIER

... Turn back to read the story of the disaster.

Location

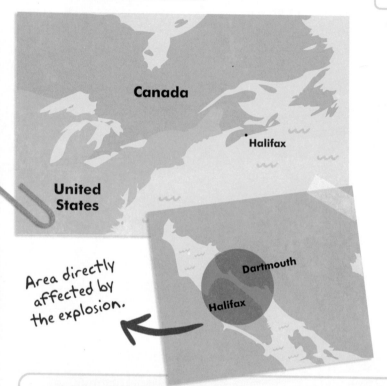

Canada

Halifax

United States

Dartmouth

Halifax

Area directly affected by the explosion.

Timeline of explosion

6 December 7.30 a.m.

SS *Mont-Blanc* heads towards the entrance of the harbour. The SS *Imo* is speeding towards the entrance in the opposite direction.

About 8.45 a.m.

The ships collide and the *Mont-Blanc* catches fire. The fire burns for 20 minutes. Many people gather on shore to watch.

Just after 9.04 a.m.

SS *Mont-Blanc* explodes with devastating force.

DEATHS AND SURVIVORS

Nearly 2,000 dead.

9,000 injured.

More than 2.5 square km (1 square mile) of Halifax flattened.

It was the BIGGEST man-made explosion ever (until the Atomic Bomb in the 1940s).

Eyewitness statements

'We saw the ship blow up, but I thought the heavens had fallen, I suppose it was because such a terrific cloud had come over. ... I looked out at the water, and absolutely everything was flying. You could see everything flying into the water.'

Dorothy Chisholm, on her way to work that morning.

'The town was literally ablaze, the dry dock and dockyard buildings completely demolished and everywhere wounded and dead.'

Frank Baker, Royal Navy sailor

'They looked like they were deliberately trying to run into each other. They had room to get by – there was no need of a collision. ... Suddenly the explosion went off.'

Barbara Orr, schoolgirl who saw the collision.

THE HALIFAX HERALD
FRIDAY, DECEMBER 7, 1917

HALIFAX WRECKED

Why were there so many deaths and injuries?

* The massive shock waves blasted the buildings and killed at least 1,600 people immediately. The glass in windows bent and then shattered, killing and injuring many more.

* A fireball of hot gas and debris shot up into the air and then rained down. Fire spread fast through wooden buildings.

* A huge 16-metre (52-foot) wave washed over the shore area. It spread over three city blocks.

Investigating and understanding

* The disaster happened during the war so at first some people thought that the explosion was caused by enemy spies.

* There were many investigations into the disaster. In 1919, an official enquiry finally decided that both the *Mont-Blanc* and the *Imo* were equally to blame.

Saving lives

* Before the war, ships leaving the harbour had to give way to ships coming in. But now there were so many ships using the port that it made it harder to stick to this rule.

* Ships leaving the harbour were supposed to keep to the right. The *Imo* was too far left, because it had already had to move out of the way of two other ships in the busy waterway.

* The captain of the *Imo* was in a hurry to get back to deliver essential supplies to Belgium. He was going too fast and he had not let the port authorities know that he was leaving the harbour.

Dangerous cargo

* A ship carrying explosives should have been flying a red flag to let other ships know it had an extremely dangerous and inflammable cargo.

* The *Mont-Blanc* was NOT flying a red flag. This was to avoid being a target for enemy submarines.

* Before the war, a boat with such a lethal cargo would not even have been allowed into the main harbour.

FOLLOW THE EXPERTS ...

The ships sounded their warning whistles. Neither of them moved out of the way of the other until it was too late.

Could the *Mont-Blanc* have sailed back out again before the 3,000 tons of explosives caught fire? The captain gave the order to abandon ship instead.

Disaster Word
annihilate

means to wipe out or destroy completely.

The Killer Lakes

Most natural disasters are caused by volcanic eruptions, earthquakes, floods and wild weather. But in the beautiful countryside of Cameroon, in Africa, there have been two, very mysterious, natural disasters.

On the night of 15 August 1984, twelve people were travelling in a truck through an area with many ancient volcanoes. Lakes have formed in some of the old volcano craters and the road went past one of them. Suddenly, the truck stopped and the driver could not start the engine no matter how hard he tried. Everyone inside the vehicle got out. Two people, who were sitting on top of the truck, watched in horror as all of them collapsed to the ground and died.

Meanwhile, in nearby villages, people were peacefully sleeping. By morning, many families woke up to find that some of their relatives had mysteriously passed away in their sleep. A total of 37 people had now died in a strange and unexplained way. Investigators were puzzled by reports of a light mist in the area. They also saw that the lake, called Lake Monoun, had turned a peculiar rusty colour. No one could explain what had happened.

Then, two years later, disaster struck again. This time it happened near another lake in Cameroon, called Lake Nyos. It was a calm, blue-coloured lake on the side of another old volcano. In the villages in the nearby valleys, many families had lived and farmed for generations.

On 21 August 1986, the peaceful lake became a killer. Very few people survived to explain what happened. Villagers were enjoying their evening meals, and settling down for the night, when they heard a strange rumbling noise. They were amazed to see a huge spout of water shooting out of their lake. Soon a vast white cloud rose into the air and spread rapidly towards them.

People gasped for air, before collapsing to the ground. All their farm animals fell down too. When the very few survivors woke up, hours later, they made an appalling discovery. They could not wake other members of their families or their neighbours. They had all died. There was a dreadful silence, because even the birds and insects had been killed. The once-beautiful Lake Nyos had turned a murky, red-brown colour.

No one had been able to explain the mysterious deaths at Lake Monoun and now there had been an even more terrible disaster. What had happened to kill so many people and animals?

Turn over to read the **disaster dossier** ...

LAKES' DISASTER DOSSIER

... Turn back to read the story of the disaster.

Location

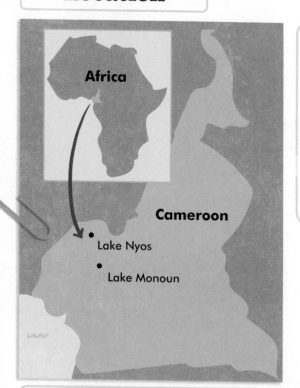

Africa

Cameroon

Lake Nyos

Lake Monoun

Lake Monoun

Date:

15 August 1984

Numbers of deaths:

37 people

Lake Nyos

Date:

21 August 1986

Numbers of deaths:

Over 1,700 people and thousands of cattle

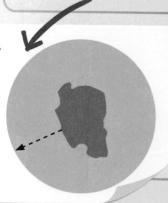

The effects of the disaster spread out from the lake for 25 km (16 miles).

Eyewitness statements

'I heard my daughter snoring in a terrible way, very abnormal. ... When crossing to my daughter's bed ... I collapsed and fell. I was there till nine o'clock in the morning ... until a friend of mine came and knocked at my door ... I wanted to speak, my breath would not come out. ... My daughter was already dead.'

'I got my motorcycle. ... A friend whose father had died left with me. ... As I rode ... through Nyos I didn't see any sign of any living thing.'

Joseph Nkwain, one of very few survivors

'Nine of us survived in my family. ... It was a stroke of luck that our house was located on a hillside ... the toxic gas did not completely envelop the hills as it did in the valleys where every living thing was killed.'

Che Kamasana Jerome, who was eight years old at the time of the disaster and lost many members of his family.

The New York Times

In Cameroon, Scenes of a Valley of Death

What killed so many people and animals?

* The mist from Lake Monoun and the white cloud from Lake Nyos were made of gases. The main gas was carbon dioxide (CO_2).

* People and animals need oxygen to breathe, but the CO_2 was like a suffocating blanket that pushed the oxygen out of the way. It asphyxiated people and animals.

* CO_2 is heavier than oxygen, so it flowed down from the lakes into the villages in the valleys below. The only survivors were people who managed to run away to higher ground.

CO_2 bursts out of lake.

Investigating and understanding

Exploding gas

* Scientists were not quite sure what had caused the deaths at Lake Monoun. After the Lake Nyos disaster they knew that a massive gas eruption must have exploded out of the lakes. It was even powerful enough to change the colour of the water.

 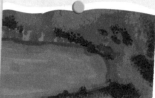

* Both lakes are in craters left behind by old volcanoes. There is magma (hot, liquid rock) deep under these lakes. It leaks carbon dioxide (CO_2) into the water.

* The CO_2 builds up at the bottom of the lakes. The water of the lakes is so calm that the CO_2 does not rise up and bubble away harmlessly. Instead, it builds up like a ticking time bomb waiting for something to trigger it.

But WHY did the gas explode out of the lakes?

'It was one of the most baffling disasters scientists have ever investigated. Lakes just don't rise up and wipe out thousands of people.'

George Kling, ecologist

Preventing disaster

* Teams of scientists have put special tubes into both lakes to let the carbon dioxide gas leak out safely. It is like letting the bubbles out of a bottle of fizzy drink, without it whooshing all over the place.

* BUT experts are worried that the rock walls around Lake Nyos might give way one day. This would not only mean the water would flood out. It would also let deadly amounts of CO_2 gas burst out again.

FOLLOW THE EXPERTS …

Limnic eruption = gas eruption from a lake.

* Scientists still DO NOT KNOW what triggered the gas to explode out of the lakes.

* There are several theories. Some geologists (rock scientists) suspect a landslide churned up the water. Others say there was a small, volcanic eruption under the lake, or that lots of rain disturbed the water.

Disaster Word
asphyxiate
means to suffocate or cut off the air we need to breathe.

Mega-eruption!

Some of the world's worst natural disasters are caused by volcanoes. One of the most destructive eruptions in human history took place on the volcanic island of Krakatau (krak-uh-taow) in Indonesia. There were probably only a few people living on Krakatau, but there were many villages on the neighbouring islands of Java and Sumatra.

The year was 1883. For many months, the people living on Java and Sumatra had been disturbed by lots of strange rumbling noises and earth tremors.

Then on Sunday 26 August, there was a sudden, sharp explosion on Krakatau. A vast, dark cloud soon covered the island. Before long, the coasts of Java and Sumatra were being pelted with hot ash and there was a red, fiery glare over Krakatau. There were more terrifying explosions, and the sea churned and pounded boats in the harbours.

Finally, on Monday morning, Krakatau exploded in a cataclysmic blast. Clouds of gas, rocks, fire and smoke shot 80 km (50 miles) up into the air. The island of Krakatau was completely destroyed. The noise from the explosion was the loudest noise EVER recorded! But, most lethal of all, the collapsing island caused terrifying sea waves called tsunamis.

The tsunamis raced along as fast as a speeding car and reached heights of up to 40 metres (130 feet). They smashed into the villages along the coasts of Java and Sumatra and destroyed everything. By the end of the day more than 36,000 people had died. Most of them were killed by these mega-tsunamis.

The effects of the terrible eruption spread all over the world over the next few months. The volcano had exploded so much ash into Earth's atmosphere that it changed the world's weather and skies. There were fiery coloured sunsets and sunrises, as well as incredible blue, green and purple light effects. Some sunsets were so vivid that in one American town the fire brigade was called to put out the 'fire'!

Krakatau was the first major world disaster to take place after the invention of the electric telegraph. Messages could now be sent all over the world using a network of cables under the seas and over land. It is amazing to think that not only did the effects of the eruption spread around the world, but so did the news of the catastrophe.

Turn over to read the **disaster dossier** ...

VOLCANO DISASTER DOSSIER

... Turn back to read the story of the disaster.

Location

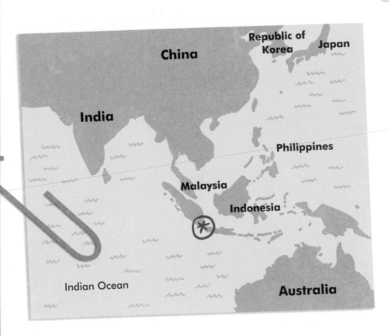

China
Republic of Korea
Japan
India
Philippines
Malaysia
Indonesia
Australia
Indian Ocean

Timeline of mega-eruption

26 August 1 p.m.
Sudden large explosion on Krakatau. Black cloud of hot ash shoots up more than 27 km (16 miles).

27 August 5.30 a.m.
More massive explosions. Huge waves batter the coasts.

27 August 10.02 a.m.
Colossal blast. Ash clouds reach up 80 km (50 miles). Krakatau explodes completely and collapses into the sea. Massive tsunamis follow.

27 August 11 p.m.
All is over. Total devastation.

DEATH AND DESTRUCTION

Over 36,000 people killed. 165 villages obliterated.

Eyewitness statements

'I am writing this blind in pitch darkness. ... So violent are the explosions that the ear-drums of over half my crew have been shattered.'
Captain Sampson, British ship *Norham Castle* off the coast of Sumatra.

'I felt a heavy pressure, throwing me to the floor. ... Then it seemed as if all the air was being sucked away and I could not breathe.'
The effect of the shock waves described by Mrs Beyerinck, Ketimbang, Sumatra.

'We saw a great black thing, a long way off, coming towards us. It was very high and very strong, and we soon saw that it was water. The people began to run for their lives.'
Man working in the rice fields of Java.

BY TELEGRAPH.

BLOTTED OUT.

Whole Villages Buried.

Mountains Submerged and Islands Made Deserts.

PEOPLE ARE KILLED
GREATEST HORROR IN THE HISTORY OF MODERN TIMES.

Towns and Villages Overwhelmed by the Lava or the Sea.

Thousands of Lives Destroyed - The Eruption Still in Progress.

Earth's surface is like a massive jigsaw made of pieces of rock called tectonic plates. They are constantly moving and there is a thick liquid of hot, melted rock called magma under them.

Why did it happen?

The most violent volcanic eruptions, like Krakatau, happen when one plate is pushed under another.

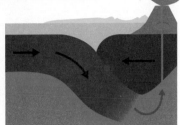

A tsunami (soo-na-mee) happens when a large amount of water is suddenly moved by an eruption or earthquake. When Krakatau exploded it caused huge tsunamis that raced across the sea to swamp other islands.

Investigating and understanding

Weird light effects

* These were caused by ash particles high up in the Earth's atmosphere.

* Meteorologists (scientists who study the weather) realized that there must be air currents carrying the ash around the planet.

* They called it the Equatorial Smoke Stream. Now we know it as the jet stream. It is like a high-speed river of air that affects climate and weather.

Predicting blasts

* Volcanologists are scientists who study volcanoes. They try to predict when and how volcanoes will erupt next.

* They look at the history of a volcano to see when it has erupted in the past.

* They take samples, record volcano temperatures and check vibrations (seismic activity) within a volcano.

Sound and shock waves

* Sounds make air molecules vibrate and change air pressure. An extremely loud sound pushes the air itself, making a shock wave that can burst your eardrums.

* The shock waves made by Krakatau spread out across the world like ripples of pressure. Scientists measured them using instruments called barometers.

* The waves were even detected as far away as London and North America. From this, the scientists understood just how loud the explosion had been.

FOLLOW THE EXPERTS ...

Disaster Word
cataclysmic
describes something that is violently destructive.

BABY VOLCANO WARNING!
Krakatau itself was destroyed in 1883, but in 1926 a new volcano called Anak Krakatau (which means 'child of Krakatau') appeared above the waves. It is growing fast and growling already!

Deadly Disease

Sometimes disasters come in the form of dreadful, killer diseases. If they spread quickly across many countries they are called pandemics.

In the fourteenth century, there were many trading routes between the different countries of the world. Merchants brought goods from China all the way to Europe and the British Isles. In October 1347, some trading ships arrived in Sicily from Asia. Sadly, everyone on board was desperately ill or already dead. Their bodies were covered in horrible, black blotches.

The sick traders and sailors were not allowed to come ashore, but no one could stop the ships' rats from scampering off into the port. They carried the disease with them. Soon, the people of Sicily were ill and dying too. The illness then spread in a deadly wave across Europe and North Africa.

The disease caused terrible black buboes (swellings) and fever. Sufferers coughed up blood and most victims died within days of falling ill. There was no known cure. By 1351, millions of people all across Europe had died. Whole communities were decimated, leaving behind abandoned buildings and empty 'ghost' villages.

People at the time did not know what caused the illness. They blamed all sorts of things like bad smells or being cursed by enemies. Modern historians call this pandemic the 'Black Death' because of the horrible black buboes. But writers at the time called it the 'Great Pestilence'.

Over the centuries, there were many other outbreaks of the same frightening disease. In 1665, it struck London and killed many thousands of people. Victims were shut up inside their homes and red crosses were painted on the door with the words 'Lord have mercy upon us'. People still thought the disease might be carried through bad air so they smoked tobacco to stop the badness getting into their lungs. Even children were told to smoke!

In the 1860s, the disease appeared again in China. Over the following years, it spread to Hong Kong and even as far as the USA. Sadly, this pandemic killed millions of people before doctors finally began to understand more about it.

Diseases like this can cause terrible disasters, so it is really important for us to discover as much as we can about them.

Turn over to read the **disaster dossier** ...

BLACK DEATH DISASTER DOSSIER

... Turn back to read the story of the disaster.

Location and timeline of disease

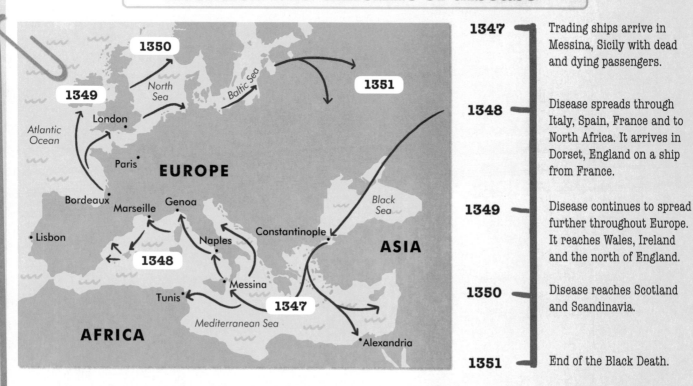

1347 Trading ships arrive in Messina, Sicily with dead and dying passengers.

1348 Disease spreads through Italy, Spain, France and to North Africa. It arrives in Dorset, England on a ship from France.

1349 Disease continues to spread further throughout Europe. It reaches Wales, Ireland and the north of England.

1350 Disease reaches Scotland and Scandinavia.

1351 End of the Black Death.

Eyewitness statements

'Those who fell sick of a kind of gross swelling of the flesh lasted for barely two days. ... It generated such horror that children did not dare visit their dying parents, nor parents their children, but fled for fear of contagion as if from leprosy or a serpent.'

John of Fordun, fourteenth-century Scottish writer

'People lay ill little more than two or three days and died suddenly. ... He who was well one day was dead the next and being carried to his grave.'

Jean de Venette, French friar, who wrote about the Black Death.

'...and finally it spread over all England and so wasted the people that scarce the tenth person of any sort was left alive.

Geoffrey the Baker, fourteenth-century English writer

NUMBER OF DEATHS

1347–1351
The Black Death killed at least one third of the population of Europe.

1665
100,000 people died in London
=
one fifth of the city's population.

Late 1800s
10 million people died in China, India and USA.

What IS this disease and WHAT causes it?

MOST LIKELY CAUSE ↓
A type of plague called BUBONIC PLAGUE.

* The rats from the trading ships had fleas on them. The fleas carried a bacterium called *Yersinia pestis*.

* The fleas bit humans and the bacteria got into their blood. This caused swellings called buboes (along with the other symptoms). That is where the name 'bubonic' plague comes from.

Bacteria are tiny, invisible organisms.

BUT some experts think the terrible disease may have been caused by another kind of germ, or virus, and not the plague bacterium.

Investigating and understanding

Digging up the past

* Historians piece together what happened during the Black Death by looking at all kinds of evidence. They read old documents written at the time and search for eyewitness descriptions.

* Archaeologists have dug up pieces of pottery from ancient rubbish dumps in villages. They can tell if they were thrown away before or after the time of the Black Death. They count the pieces and this shows how many people were alive to use the pottery before and after the pandemic.

Disease ID

* The bacterium that caused bubonic plague was found in 1894 by a French-Swiss doctor called Alexandre Yersin and a Japanese doctor, Kitasato Shibasaburo. It was named *Yersinia pestis* after Yersin.

* Epidemiologists are scientists who study what causes diseases and how they spread. They have tested the bones and teeth of Black Death victims from burial pits and found *Yersinia pestis*.

Preventing pandemics

* Modern medicines, like antibiotics, are used to cure cases of plague now. In earlier times, doctors tried some very weird treatments and they also wore strange outfits to try to avoid catching it themselves!

* Nowadays, there are ways of controlling rats and fleas to prevent them from passing on harmful bacteria to humans.

* Health organizations, like the World Health Organization (WHO), work very hard to treat and prevent the spread of any dangerous diseases.

Scary beak mask worn by doctors in the 1600s.

FOLLOW THE EXPERTS ...

* All of this research is so important as it helps us to understand the way the disease spread across countries. This expert knowledge can help to protect us in the future.

Disaster Word
decimate
means to kill or destroy a large number of people.

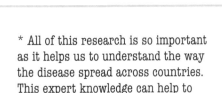

Leabharlanna Poiblí Chathair Baile Átha Cliath
Dublin City Public Libraries

Deadly Disease

DISASTER WORDS EXPLAINED

Annihilate means to wipe out or destroy completely.

Antibiotic is a kind of medicine that can be used to treat diseases and infections caused by bacteria.

Asphyxiate means to suffocate or cut off the air we need to breathe.

Bacterium is a tiny, invisible organism. 'Bacteria' is the word for more than one. Some bacteria cause diseases.

Bioluminescent describes a small organism or creature that makes its own light. Bioluminescent sea creatures make the water glow!

Buboes are painful swellings on the thighs, neck, armpit or groin. They are a symptom of bubonic plague.

Cataclysmic means something that is violently destructive.

Catastrophic describes something that causes huge damage or suffering.

Climate is not the same as weather. The weather can change in just a few hours. Climate changes over hundreds, or millions, of years.

Colossal describes something that is really enormous.

Decimate means to kill or destroy a large number of people.

Devastate means to destroy something completely.

Extinction means dying out completely. If a species of animal is extinct, there is not one of them left alive in the whole world.

Hypothermia is when you get so cold it can kill you.

Inferno is a very large fire that is out of control.

Inflammable describes something that bursts into flames very easily.

Inundate means to flood an area with water.

Landslide is when a part of a hill, cliff or mountain collapses. Mud, rocks and earth slide down.

Lethal describes something that is so dangerous it can kill you.

Obliterate means to destroy entirely.

Pandemic is an outbreak of disease that spreads across many countries, or even the whole world.

Perilous means extremely dangerous.

Premonition is a strong feeling that something unpleasant or horrible is about to happen.

Shrapnel is small pieces of metal from exploding bombs and shells.

Supernatural describes something that cannot be explained by what we know about the world around us.

Tsunami is when a huge amount of water is suddenly moved by a volcanic eruption, earthquake or explosion. It makes an enormous, deadly wave.

Virus is a tiny, invisible organism that is smaller than a bacterium. It causes diseases like colds and chickenpox. It cannot be treated with antibiotic medicine.